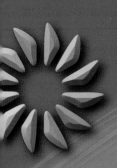

DISCOVER
SEA HORSES

by Helen Foster James

Cherry Lake Publishing • Ann Arbor, Michigan

3

Published in the United States of America
by Cherry Lake Publishing
Ann Arbor, Michigan
www.cherrylakepublishing.com

Content Adviser: Dominique A. Didier, PhD, Associate Professor,
Department of Biology, Millersville University
Reading Adviser: Marla Conn, ReadAbility, Inc

Photo Credits: © Mariusz Niedzwiedzki/Shutterstock Images, cover, 20;
© Tambako the Jaguar/Flickr Images, 4, 12; James van den Broek/Shutterstock
Images, 6; ©Kristina Vackova/Shutterstock Images, 8, 10; © huxiaohua/
Shutterstock Images, 14; © Kirt Peart Professional Imaging/Shutterstock
Images, 16; © nicolas.voisin44/Shutterstock Images, 18

Library of Congress Cataloging-in-Publication Data
James, Helen Foster, 1951-author.
  Discover sea horses / Helen Foster James.
       pages cm.—(Splash!)
  Audience: Ages 6–10
  Audience: K to grade 3
  Includes bibliographical references and index.
  ISBN 978-1-63362-605-8 (hardcover)—ISBN 978-1-63362-695-9 (pbk.)
—ISBN 978-1-63362-785-7 (pdf)—ISBN
978-1-63362-875-5 (ebook)
  1. Sea horses—Juvenile literature. I. Title. II. Title: Sea horses.

  QL638.S9J325 2016
  597.6798—dc23
                                        2015000583

Cherry Lake Publishing would like to acknowledge the work of the Partnership for
21st Century Skills. Please visit www.p21.org for more information.

Printed in the United States of America
Corporate Graphics

TABLE OF CONTENTS

Unusual Fish

A sea horse is not a horse. It is a fish!

Sea horses use **gills** to breathe. They live in water. **Fins** help them swim.

One fin is on their back. Two small fins are found beneath their gills on the back of the head.

The gills are in a pouch under the cheek of this sea horse.

Sea horses have a long **snout**. They use it like a straw. They suck in tiny sea life that floats by.

THINK!

Sea horses swim upright and are slower swimmers than other fish. Why do you think this is?

Sea horses pull in food with their snouts.

Sea horses wrap their tails around sea plants. They use their **prehensile** tails to stay in place.

This sea horse is curling its tail around a plant.

Cool Coronets

Sea horses have an unusual shape.

They have fleshy bumps that form a **coronet** on their head. No two coronets are the same.

LOOK! Look at the colors and patterns on this sea horse. What would be a good nickname for this animal?

Sea horses have coronets on top of their heads.

A sea horse's eyes can look forward and backward at the same time.

MAKE A GUESS!

Why is it helpful for sea horses to have eyes that can look in different directions?

Sea horses' eyes are not like the eyes of other animals.

Sea horse dads give birth to babies. They have hundreds of **fry** at one time.

Unlike most animals, the sea horse males are the ones who give birth.

Sea horses can change color. This is how they **camouflage** themselves. They blend in with their surroundings. This keeps them safe.

Sea horses can change the colors of their skin.

Protecting Sea Horses

People need to protect sea horses. If you see a sea horse, leave it alone. Keeping oceans clean protects their **habitat**.

If you touch a sea horse, you could injure it.

Scientists are still learning about sea horses. There is much to study about this unusual fish.

CREATE! Make a list of five unusual sea horse facts. Share what you know with a friend.

Sea horses look very different than other fish.

Think About It

Jacques Cousteau was a famous ocean explorer. He once said, "People protect what they love." How can you help protect sea horses? Do you want to learn more about sea horses? Visit your library to learn more facts and see more photographs.

Why do you think people are so fascinated by sea horses?

How can you help keep oceans clean for sea horses?

Find Out More

BOOK

Bell, Samantha. *Sea Horses*. Ann Arbor, MI: Cherry Lake Publishing, 2014.

WEB SITE

Monterey Bay Aquarium—Behind the Scenes at the Seahorse Exhibit

http://montereybayaquarium.tumblr.com/post/49537822982/behind-the-scenes-at-the-seahorse-exhibit

The aquarium takes Web visitors behind the scenes of its sea horse exhibit.

Glossary

camouflage (KAM-uh-flahzh) to change color or shape to blend in with surroundings

coronet (kor-uh-NET) another word for crown

fins (FINZ) parts on the body of a sea creature shaped like flaps that are used for moving and steering through the water

fry (FRYE) baby sea horses

gills (GILZ) organs near a fish's mouth used for breathing

habitat (HAB-ih-tat) place where a plant or animal naturally lives

prehensile (pree-HEN-syle) able to grasp an object

snout (snout) the long front part of an animal's head, which includes the nose, mouth, and jaws

Index

About the Author

Dr. Helen Foster James likes to read, write, travel, and hike in the mountains with her friends. She visited a sea horse farm where a sea horse wrapped its tail around her finger. She lives by the Pacific Ocean in San Diego, California, with her husband, Bob.